Celebrate Rec

Stepping Out of Denial into God's Grace

The Journey Begins

PARTICIPANT'S GUIDE 1

John Baker is the founder of Celebrate Recovery®, a ministry started at Saddleback Church. It is estimated that over the last 25 years more than 1.5 million people have gone through this Christ-centered recovery program. There are currently over 27,000 churches that have weekly Celebrate Recovery meetings.

John has been on staff since Celebrate Recovery started. He has served as the Pastor of Membership, the Pastor of Ministries, and is currently the Pastor of Saddleback Church's Signature Ministries. He is also serving as one of the nine Elder Pastors at Saddleback. John is a nationally known speaker and trainer in helping churches start Celebrate Recovery ministries.

John's writing accomplishments include Celebrate Recovery's *The Journey Begins* Curriculum, *Life's Healing Choices*, the *Celebrate Recovery Study Bible* (general editor), and *The Landing* and *Celebration Place* (coauthor). John's newest books are *Your First Step to Celebrate Recovery* and *The Celebrate Recovery Devotional* (coauthor).

John and his wife Cheryl, the cofounder of Celebrate Recovery, have been married for more than four decades and have served together in Celebrate Recovery since the beginning. They have two adult children, Laura and Johnny, and five grandchildren.

Johnny Baker has been on staff at Celebrate Recovery since 2004 and has been the Pastor of Celebrate Recovery at Saddleback Church since 2012. As an adult child of an alcoholic who chose to become an alcoholic himself, Johnny is passionate about breaking the cycle of dysfunction in his family and helping other families find the tools that will lead to healing and openness. He knows that because of Jesus Christ, and by continuing to stay active in Celebrate Recovery, Maggie, Chloe, and Jimmy—his three children—will never see him drink. Johnny is a nationally recognized speaker, trainer, and teacher of Celebrate Recovery. He is a coauthor of the *Celebrate Recovery Daily Devotional*, *Celebration Place*, and *The Landing*, and is an associate editor of the *Celebrate Recovery Study Bible*. He has been married since 2000 to his wife Jeni, who serves alongside him in Celebrate Recovery.

REVISED EDITION

Celebrate Recovery®

Stepping Out of Denial into God's Grace

PARTICIPANT'S GUIDE 1

The Journey Begins

A recovery program based on
eight principles from the Beatitudes

JOHN BAKER

FOREWORD BY RICK WARREN

ZONDERVAN®

ZONDERVAN

Stepping Out of Denial into God's Grace

Requests for information should be addressed to:
Zondervan, 3900 *Sparks Drive SE, Grand Rapids, Michigan 49546*

ISBN: 978-0-310-13138-0 (softcover)
ISBN: 978-0-310-13139-7 (ebook)

Interior design: Michelle Espinoza

Printed in the United States of America

Contents

Foreword by Rick Warren

You've undoubtedly heard the expression "Time heals all wounds." Unfortunately, it isn't true. As a pastor I frequently talk with people who are still carrying hurts from thirty or forty years ago. The truth is, time often makes things worse. Wounds that are left untended fester and spread infection throughout your entire body. Time only extends the pain if the problem isn't dealt with.

Celebrate Recovery® is a biblical and balanced program that can help you overcome your hurts, habits, and hang-ups. Based on the actual words of Jesus rather than psychological theory, this recovery program is more effective in helping people change than anything else I've seen or heard of. Over the years I've witnessed how the Holy Spirit has used this program to transform literally thousands of lives at Saddleback Church and help people grow toward full Christlike maturity.

Perhaps you are familiar with the classic 12-Step program of AA and other groups. While undoubtedly many lives have been helped through the 12 Steps, I've always been uncomfortable with that program's vagueness about the nature of God, the saving power of Jesus Christ, and the ministry of the Holy Spirit. So I began an intense study of the Scriptures to discover what God had to say about "recovery." To my amazement, I found the principles of recovery — in their logical order — given by Christ in His most famous message, the Sermon on the Mount.

My study resulted in a ten-week series of messages called "The Road to Recovery." During that series my associate pastor John Baker developed the four participant's guides, which became the heart of our Celebrate Recovery program.

As you work through these participant's guides, I trust that you will come to realize many benefits from this program. Most of all, however, my prayer for you is that, through Celebrate Recovery, you will find deep peace and lasting freedom in Jesus Christ as you walk your own road to recovery.

Dr. Rick Warren
Senior Pastor, Saddleback Church

Introduction

Welcome to the "Road to Recovery." You are in for an exciting and amazing journey as you take the hand of the true and only Higher Power, Jesus Christ, and walk with Him toward healing and serenity.

The purpose of this program is to allow us to become free from life's hurts, hang-ups, and habits. By working through the eight recovery principles found in the Beatitudes with Jesus Christ as your Higher Power, you can and will change! You will begin to experience the true peace and serenity you have been seeking, and you will no longer have to rely on your dysfunctional, compulsive, and addictive behaviors as a temporary "fix" for your pain.

By applying the biblical principles of conviction, conversion, surrender, confession, restitution, prayer, quiet time, witnessing, and helping one another, which are found within the eight principles and the Christ-centered 12 Steps, you will restore and develop stronger relationships with others and with God.

To begin our journey, we will need to step out of denial and into God's grace. This is what working through Principles 1 – 3 will help us accomplish. We begin by looking at the toll *denial* has had on our ability to face the reality of our past and present. Then we need to admit that we are *powerless* over certain areas of our lives, and that, alone, we do not have the power to control them.

In Principle 2, we find the *hope* that our Higher Power, Jesus Christ, can restore us to *sanity* and that through Him alone we can find the power to help us recover. And finally, in Principle 3, we take the *action* to *turn* our lives and our wills over to His care and direction.

After each lesson, there is an exercise for you to complete. Answer each question to the best of your ability. Don't worry about what you think the answer *should* be. Pray and then write down the answer from your heart. Remember John 8:32: "Then you will know the truth, and the truth will set you free."

After you have completed the exercise, share it with someone you trust. Your group, an accountability partner, your sponsor (someone farther along in recovery who has agreed to be your "travel guide"; sponsors are explained in Participant's Guide 2, Lesson 7), or a close friend in recovery are all choices. You do not recover from your hurts, hang-ups, and habits just by attending recovery meetings. You must work and live following the eight principles of recovery found in the Beatitudes and the 12 Steps and their biblical comparisons. God bless you as you walk this road.

In His steps,
John Baker

The Road to Recovery

Eight Principles Based on the Beatitudes

By Pastor Rick Warren

1. **R**ealize I'm not God. I admit that I am powerless to control my tendency to do the wrong thing and that my life is unmanageable.
   "Happy are those who know they are spiritually poor."
   (Matthew 5:3)
2. **E**arnestly believe that God exists, that I matter to Him, and that He has the power to help me recover.
   "Happy are those who mourn, for they shall be comforted."
   (Matthew 5:4)
3. **C**onsciously choose to commit all my life and will to Christ's care and control.
   "Happy are the meek." (Matthew 5:5)
4. **O**penly examine and confess my faults to myself, to God, and to someone I trust.
   "Happy are the pure in heart." (Matthew 5:8)
5. **V**oluntarily submit to every change God wants to make in my life and humbly ask Him to remove my character defects.
   "Happy are those whose greatest desire is to do what God requires."
   (Matthew 5:6)
6. **E**valuate all my relationships. Offer forgiveness to those who have hurt me and make amends for harm I've done to others, except when to do so would harm them or others.
   "Happy are the merciful." (Matthew 5:7)
   "Happy are the peacemakers." (Matthew 5:9)
7. **R**eserve a daily time with God for self-examination, Bible reading, and prayer in order to know God and His will for my life and to gain the power to follow His will.
8. **Y**ield myself to God to be used to bring this Good News to others, both by my example and by my words.
   "Happy are those who are persecuted because they do what God requires." (Matthew 5:10)

Twelve Steps and Their Biblical Comparisons*

1. We admitted we were powerless over our addictions and compulsive behaviors, that our lives had become unmanageable.

   "For I know that good itself does not dwell in me, that is, in my sinful nature. For I have the desire to do what is good, but I cannot carry it out." (Romans 7:18)

2. We came to believe that a power greater than ourselves could restore us to sanity.

   "For it is God who works in you to will and to act in order to fulfill his good purpose." (Philippians 2:13)

3. We made a decision to turn our lives and our wills over to the care of God.

   "Therefore, I urge you, brothers and sisters, in view of God's mercy, to offer your bodies as a living sacrifice, holy and pleasing to God — this is your true and proper worship." (Romans 12:1)

4. We made a searching and fearless moral inventory of ourselves.

   "Let us examine our ways and test them, and let us return to the LORD." (Lamentations 3:40)

5. We admitted to God, to ourselves, and to another human being the exact nature of our wrongs.

   "Therefore confess your sins to each other and pray for each other so that you may be healed." (James 5:16)

6. We were entirely ready to have God remove all these defects of character.

   "Humble yourselves before the Lord, and he will lift you up." (James 4:10)

7. We humbly asked Him to remove all our shortcomings.

   "If we confess our sins, he is faithful and just and will forgive us our sins and purify us from all unrighteousness." (1 John 1:9)

8. We made a list of all persons we had harmed and became willing to make amends to them all.

   "Do to others as you would have them do to you." (Luke 6:31)

9. We made direct amends to such people whenever possible, except when to do so would injure them or others.

   "Therefore, if you are offering your gift at the altar and there remember that your brother or sister has something against you, leave your gift there in front of the altar. First go and be reconciled to them; then come and offer your gift." (Matthew 5:23 – 24)

10. We continued to take personal inventory and when we were wrong, promptly admitted it.

    "So, if you think you are standing firm, be careful that you don't fall!" (1 Corinthians 10:12)

11. We sought through prayer and meditation to improve our conscious contact with God, praying only for knowledge of His will for us and power to carry that out.

    "Let the message of Christ dwell among you richly." (Colossians 3:16)

12. Having had a spiritual experience as the result of these steps, we try to carry this message to others and to practice these principles in all our affairs.

    "Brothers and sisters, if someone is caught in a sin, you who live by the Spirit should restore that person gently. But watch yourselves, or you also may be tempted." (Galatians 6:1)

* Throughout this material, you will notice several references to the Christ-centered 12 Steps. Our prayer is that Celebrate Recovery will create a bridge to the millions of people who are familiar with the secular 12 Steps (I acknowledge the use of some material from the 12 Suggested Steps of Alcoholics Anonymous) and in so doing, introduce them to the one and only true Higher Power, Jesus Christ. Once they begin that relationship, asking Christ into their hearts as Lord and Savior, true healing and recovery can begin!

Serenity Prayer

If you have attended secular recovery programs, you have seen the first four lines of the "Prayer for Serenity." The following is the complete prayer. I encourage you to pray it daily as you work through the principles!

Prayer for Serenity

God, grant me the serenity
to accept the things I cannot change,
the courage to change the things I can,
and the wisdom to know the difference.
Living one day at a time,
enjoying one moment at a time ;
accepting hardship as a pathway to peace ;
taking, as Jesus did,
this sinful world as it is,
not as I would have it ;
trusting that You will make all things right
if I surrender to Your will ;
so that I may be reasonably happy in this life
and supremely happy with You forever in the next.
Amen.

Reinhold Niebuhr

Celebrate Recovery's Small Group Guidelines

The following five guidelines will ensure that your small group is a safe place. They need to be read at the beginning of every meeting.

1. Keep your sharing focused on your own thoughts and feelings. Limit your sharing to three to five minutes.
2. There is NO cross talk. Cross talk is when two individuals engage in conversation excluding all others. Each person is free to express his or her feelings without interruptions.
3. We are here to support one another, not "fix" another.
4. Anonymity and confidentiality are basic requirements. What is shared in the group stays in the group. The only exception is when someone threatens to injure themselves or others.
5. Offensive language has no place in a Christ-centered recovery group.

Denial

Principle 1: Realize I'm not God. I admit that I am powerless to control my tendency to do the wrong thing and that my life is unmanageable.

"Happy are those who know they are spiritually poor." (Matthew 5:3)

Step 1: We admitted we were powerless over our addictions and compulsive behaviors, that our lives had become unmanageable.

"For I know that good itself does not dwell in me, that is, in my sinful nature. For I have the desire to do what is good, but I cannot carry it out." (Romans 7:18)

Think About It

Before we can take the first step of our recovery, we must first face and admit our denial.

God tells us, "You can't heal a wound by saying it's not there!" (Jeremiah 6:14, TLB). The acrostic for DENIAL spells out what can happen if we do not face our denial.

Disables our feelings

By repressing our feelings we freeze our emotions. Understanding and feeling our feelings is freedom.

"They promise them freedom, while they themselves are slaves of destructive habits — for we are slaves of anything that has conquered us." (2 Peter 2:19, GNT)

Energy lost

A side effect of our denial is anxiety. Anxiety causes us to waste precious energy running from our past and worrying about and dreading the future. It is only in the present, today, where positive change can occur.

"He frees the prisoners . . .; he lifts the burdens from those bent down beneath their loads." (Psalm 146:7 – 8, TLB)

Negates growth

We are "as sick as our secrets." We cannot grow in recovery until we are ready to step out of our denial into the truth.

"They cried to the Lord in their troubles, and he rescued them! He led them from their darkness and shadow of death and snapped their chains." (Psalm 107:13 – 14, TLB)

Isolates us from God

God's light shines on the truth. Our denial keeps us in the dark.

"God is light; in him there is no darkness at all. If we claim to have fellowship with him yet walk in the darkness, we lie and do not live out the truth. But if we walk in the light, as he is in the light, we have fellowship with one another, and the blood of Jesus, his Son, purifies us from all sin." (1 John 1:5 – 7)

Alienates us from our relationships

Denial tells us we are getting away with it. We think no one knows — but they do.

What is the answer?

"Stop lying to each other; tell the truth, for we are parts of each other and when we lie to each other we are hurting ourselves."
(Ephesians 4:25, TLB)

Lengthens the pain

We have the false belief that denial protects us from our pain. In reality, denial allows our pain to fester and grow and turn into *shame* and *guilt.*

God's promise: "I will give you back your health again and heal your wounds." (Jeremiah 30:17, TLB)

Accept the first principle of recovery. Step out of your denial! Step into your Higher Power's — Jesus Christ's — unconditional love and grace!

Write About It

1. What areas of your life do you have power (control) over? Be specific.

2. What areas of your life are out of control, unmanageable? Be specific.

3. How do you think taking this first step will help you?

4. As a child, what coping skills did you use to get attention or to protect yourself?

5. In your family of origin, what was the "family secret" that everyone was trying to protect?

6. How do you handle pain and disappointment?

7. How can you begin to address your denial?

8. In what areas of your life are you now beginning to face reality and break the effects of denial?

9. Are you starting to develop a support team? Are you asking for phone numbers in your meetings?

   List them here or on the inside back cover of this participant's guide!

Powerless

Principle 1: Realize I'm not God. I admit that I am powerless to control my tendency to do the wrong thing and that my life is unmanageable."

"Happy are those who know they are spiritually poor." (Matthew 5:3)

Step 1: We admitted we were powerless over our addictions and compulsive behaviors, that our lives had become unmanageable.

"For I know that good itself does not dwell in me, that is, in my sinful nature. For I have the desire to do what is good, but I cannot carry it out." (Romans 7:18)

Think About It

When we accept the first recovery principle and take that first step out of our denial and into reality, we see there are very few things that we really have control over. Once we admit that by ourselves we are powerless we can stop living with the following "serenity robbers," spelled out in the acrostic POWERLESS.

Pride

Ignorance + power + pride = a deadly mixture!

"Pride ends in a fall, while humility brings honor." (Proverbs 29:23, TLB)

Only ifs

Our "only ifs" in life keep us trapped in the fantasyland of rationalization!

"Whatever is covered up will be uncovered, and every secret will be made known. So then, whatever you have said in the dark will be heard in broad daylight." (Luke 12:2 – 3, GNT)

Worry

Worrying is a form of not trusting God enough!

"So don't be anxious about tomorrow. God will take care of your tomorrow too. Live one day at a time." (Matthew 6:34, TLB)

Escape

By living in denial we may have escaped into a world of fantasy and unrealistic expectations of ourselves and others.

"For light is capable of showing up everything for what it really is. It is even possible for light to turn the thing it shines upon into light also." (Ephesians 5:13 – 14, PH)

Resentments

Resentments act like an emotional cancer if they are allowed to fester and grow.

"'In your anger do not sin': Do not let the sun go down while you are still angry, and do not give the devil a foothold." (Ephesians 4:26 – 27)

Loneliness

Loneliness is a choice. In recovery and in Christ, you never have to walk alone.

"Continue to love each other with true brotherly love. Don't forget to be kind to strangers, for some who have done this have entertained angels without realizing it!" (Hebrews 13:1 – 2, TLB)

Emptiness

You know that empty feeling deep inside. The cold wind of hopelessness blows right through it.

Jesus said, "My purpose is to give life in all its fullness." (John 10:10, TLB)

Selfishness

We often pray: "Our Father which art in heaven; give me, give me, give me."

"Whoever clings to his life shall lose it, and whoever loses his life shall save it." (Luke 17:33, TLB)

Separation

Some people talk about finding God — as if He could ever get lost!

"For I am convinced that nothing can ever separate us from his love. Death can't, and life can't. The angels won't, and all the powers of hell itself cannot keep God's love away. . . . Nothing will ever be able to separate us from the love God demonstrated by our Lord Jesus Christ when he died for us." (Romans 8:38 – 39, TLB)

Congratulations! In your admission of your powerlessness you have begun the journey of recovery that will allow you to accept the true and only Higher Power's — Jesus Christ's — healing, love, and forgiveness.

At this stage in your recovery, you need to *stop* doing two things:

1. Stop Denying the Pain

You are ready to take your first step in recovery when your pain is greater than your fear.

"Pity me, O Lord, for I am weak. Heal me, for my body is sick, and I am upset and disturbed. My mind is filled with apprehension and with gloom." (Psalm 6:2 – 3, TLB)

2. Stop Playing God

You are unable to do for yourself what you need God to do for you. You are either going to serve God or yourself. You can't serve both.

"You cannot be a slave of two masters; you will hate one and love the other; you will be loyal to one and despise the other." (Matthew 6:24, GNT)

In addition to stopping certain behaviors, you need to start doing two things:

1. Start Admitting Your Powerlessness

As you work the first principle, you will see that by yourself you do not have the power to change your hurts, hang-ups, and habits.

"Jesus . . . said, 'With man this is impossible, but with God all things are possible.' " (Matthew 19:26)

2. Start Admitting That Your Life Has Become Unmanageable

You can finally start admitting that some or all areas of your life are out of your control to change.

"Problems far too big for me to solve are piled higher than my head. Meanwhile my sins, too many to count, have all caught up with me and I am ashamed to look up." (Psalm 40:12, TLB).

Principle 1 Prayer

Dear God, Your Word tells me that I can't heal my hurts, hang-ups, and habits by just saying that they are not there. Help me! Parts of my life, or all of my life, are out of control. I now know that I cannot "fix" myself. It seems the harder that I try to do the right thing the more I struggle. Lord, I want to step out of my denial into the truth. I pray for You to show me the way. In Your Son's name I pray, Amen.

Note: Before you begin "Write About It," read the "Prayer for Serenity" on page 14 and read the Principle 1 verses on page 31.

Write About It

1. List some of the ways that your pride has stopped you from asking for and getting the help you need to overcome your hurts, hang-ups, and habits.

2. What in your past has caused you to have the "if onlys"?

   "If only" I had stopped ______________________ years ago.

   "If only" ______________________ hadn't left me.

3. Instead of worrying about things that we cannot control, we need to focus on what God can do in our lives. What are you worrying about? Why?

4. In what ways have you tried to escape your past pain? Be specific.

5. How has holding on to your anger and your resentments affected you?

6. Do you believe that loneliness is a choice? Why or why not? How has your denial isolated you from your important relationships?

7. Describe the emptiness you feel and some new ways you are finding to fill it?

8. Selfishness is at the heart of most problems between people. In what areas of your life have you been selfish?

9. Separation from God can feel very real, but it is never permanent. What can you do to get closer to God?

Principle 1 Verses

"You can't heal a wound by saying it's not there!"
(Jeremiah 6:14, TLB)

"If you wait for perfect conditions, you will never get anything done." (Ecclesiastes 11:4, TLB)

"My heart is troubled and restless. Waves of affliction have come upon me." (Job 30:27 TLB)

"I don't understand myself at all, for I really want to do what is right, but I can't. I do what I don't want to — what I hate. I know perfectly well that what I am doing is wrong, and my bad conscience proves that I agree with these laws I am breaking. But I can't help myself, because I'm no longer doing it. It is sin inside me that is stronger than I am that makes me do these evil things."
(Romans 7:15 – 17, TLB)

"Before every man there lies a wide and pleasant road that seems right but ends in death." (Proverbs 14:12, TLB)

"My good days are in the past. My hopes have disappeared. My heart's desires are broken." (Job 17:11, TLB)

"I am worn out with pain; every night my pillow is wet with tears. My eyes are growing old and dim with grief because of all my enemies." (Psalm 6:6 – 7, TLB)

"We felt we were doomed to die and saw how powerless we were to help ourselves." (2 Corinthians 1:9, TLB)

Lesson 3

HOPE

Principle 2: Earnestly believe that God exists, that I matter to Him, and that He has the power to help me recover.

"Happy are those who mourn, for they shall be comforted." (Matthew 5:4)

Step 2: We came to believe that a power greater than ourselves could restore us to sanity.

"For it is God who works in you to will and to act in order to fulfill his good purpose." (Philippians 2:13)

Think About It

"Anyone who comes to [God] must believe that he exists and that he rewards those who earnestly seek him." (Hebrews 11:6)

In the first principle, we admitted we were powerless. Now in the second principle, we come to believe God exists, that we are important to Him, and that we are able to receive God's power to help us recover. It's in the second step we find HOPE!

Higher Power

Our Higher Power has a name: Jesus Christ! Jesus desires a hands-on, day-to-day, moment-to-moment relationship with us. He can do for us what we have never been able to do for ourselves.

"Everything comes from God alone. Everything lives by his power." (Romans 11:36, TLB)

Our Higher Power tells us, "My grace is enough for you: for where there is weakness, my power is shown the more completely." (2 Corinthians 12:9, PH)

Openness to change

Throughout our lives, we will continue to encounter hurts and trials that we are powerless to change. With God's help, we need to be open to allow those trials to change us. To make us better, not bitter.

"Now your attitudes and thoughts must all be constantly changing for the better. Yes, you must be a new and different person." (Ephesians 4:23, TLB)

Power to change

In the past, we have wanted to change and were unable to do so. We could not free ourselves from our hurts, hang-ups, or habits. In Principle 2, we come to understand that God's power can change us and our situation.

"For I can do everything God asks me to with the help of Christ who gives me the strength and the power." (Philippians 4:13, TLB)

"Lead me; teach me; for you are the God who gives me salvation. I have no hope except in you." (Psalm 25:5, TLB)

Expect to change

Remember you are only at the second principle. Don't quit before the miracle happens! With God's help, the changes that you have longed for are just *steps* away.

"I am sure that God who began the good work within you will keep right on helping you grow in his grace until his task within you is

finally finished on that day when Jesus Christ returns." (Philippians 1:6, TLB)

How do we find hope? By faith in our Higher Power, Jesus Christ.

"Now faith is confidence in what we hope for and assurance about what we do not see." (Hebrews 11:1)

Write About It

1. Before taking this step, where were you trying to find hope?

2. What do you believe about God? What are some of His characteristics?

3. How are your feelings for your heavenly Father and your earthly father alike? How do they differ?

4. How can your relationship with your Higher Power, Jesus Christ, help you step out of your denial and face reality?

5. In what areas of your life are you now ready to let God help you?

6. What things are you ready to change in your life? Where can you get the power to change them?

Lesson 4

SANITY

Principle 2: Earnestly believe that God exists, that I matter to Him, and that He has the power to help me recover.

"Happy are those who mourn, for they shall be comforted." (Matthew 5:4)

Step 2: We came to believe that a power greater than ourselves could restore us to sanity.

"For it is God who works in you to will and to act in order to fulfill his good purpose." (Philippians 2:13)

Think About It

Insanity has been described as "doing the same thing over and over again, expecting a different result each time."

Sanity has been defined as "wholeness of mind; making decisions based on the truth."

The following are some of the gifts we will receive when we believe that our Higher Power, Jesus Christ, has the power and will restore us to SANITY!

Strength

Jesus gives us strength to face the fears that in the past have caused us to fight, flee, or freeze.

"God is our refuge and our strength, an ever-present help in trouble. Therefore we will not fear." (Psalm 46:1)

"My mind and my body may grow weak, but God is my strength; he is all I ever need." (Psalm 73:26, GNT)

Acceptance

We learn to have realistic expectations of ourselves and others.

"Accept one another, then, for the glory of God, as Christ has accepted you." (Romans 15:7, GNT)

New life

We discover that we have an opportunity for a second chance! We do not have to live by our old ways any longer.

"When someone becomes a Christian he becomes a brand new person inside. He is not the same anymore. A new life has begun!" (2 Corinthians 5:17, TLB)

Integrity

We begin to follow through on our promises. Others start trusting what we say.

"Nothing brings me greater joy than hearing that my children are living in the truth." (3 John 4, PH)

Trust

We begin to trust relationships with others and our Higher Power, Jesus Christ!

"It is dangerous to be concerned with what others think of you, but if you trust the Lord, you are safe." (Proverbs 29:25, GNT)

Your Higher Power, Jesus Christ, loves you just the way you are!

No matter what you have done in the past, God wants to forgive it!

"While we were still sinners, Christ died for us." (Romans 5:8)

No matter what shape your life is in today, together God and you can handle it!

"And God is faithful; he will not let you be tempted beyond what you can bear. But when you are tempted, he will also provide a way out." (1 Corinthians 10:13)

And if you take action to complete the next principle, your future will be blessed and secure!

"So don't be anxious about tomorrow. God will take care of your tomorrow too. Live one day at a time." (Matthew 6:34, TLB)

Principle 2 Prayer

Dear God, I have tried to "fix" and "control" my life's hurts, hang-ups, or habits all by myself. I admit that, by myself, I am powerless to change. I need to begin to believe and receive Your power to help me recover. You loved me enough to send Your Son to the cross to die for my sins. Help me be open to the hope that I can only find in Him. Please help me to start living my life one day at a time. In Jesus' name I pray, Amen.

Write About It

1. What things have you been doing over and over again, expecting a different result each time (insanity)?

2. What is your definition of sanity?

3. How have your past expectations of yourself or others been unrealistic? Give examples.

4. In the past, how has trusting only in your own feelings and emotions gotten you in trouble?

5. How can your Higher Power, Jesus Christ, help restore you to make sane decisions? How do you get a second chance?

6. What areas of your life are you ready to release control of and hand over to God? Be specific.

Principle 2 Verses

"Remember that in the past you were without Christ. You were not citizens of Israel, and you had no part in the agreements with the promise that God made to his people. You had no hope, and you did not know God. But now in Christ Jesus, you who were far away from God are brought near through the blood of Christ's death."
(Ephesians 2:12 – 13, NCV)

"But this precious treasure — this light and power that now shine within us — is held in a perishable container, that is, in our weak bodies. Everyone can see that the glorious power within must be from God and is not our own. We are pressed on every side by troubles, but not crushed and broken. We are perplexed because we don't know why things happen as they do, but we don't give up and quit."
(2 Corinthians 4:7 – 8, TLB)

"And this is the secret: that Christ in your hearts is your only hope of glory." (Colossians 1:27, TLB)

"Don't copy the behavior and customs of this world, but be a new and different person with a fresh newness in all you do and think. Then you will learn from your own experience how his ways will really satisfy you." (Romans 12:2, TLB)

"He will not break the bruised reed, nor quench the dimly burning flame. He will encourage the fainthearted, those tempted to despair. He will see full justice given to all who have been wronged."
(Isaiah 42:3, TLB)

Lesson 5

TURN

Principle 3: Consciously choose to commit all my life and will to Christ's care and control.

"Happy are the meek." (Matthew 5:5)

Step 3: We made a decision to turn our lives and our wills over to the care of God.

"Therefore, I urge you, brothers and sisters, in view of God's mercy, to offer your bodies as a living sacrifice, holy and pleasing to God — this is your true and proper worship." (Romans 12:1)

Think About It

How do you TURN your life over to the one and only Higher Power, Jesus Christ?

Trust

Deciding to turn your life and your will over to God requires only trust. Trust is putting the faith you found in Principle 2 into action.

"If you confess that Jesus is Lord and believe that God raised him from death, you will be saved." (Romans 10:9, GNT)

Understand

Relying solely on your own understanding got you into recovery in the first place! After you make the decision to ask Jesus into your life, you need to begin to seek His will for your life in all your decisions.

"Trust in the LORD with all your heart and lean not on your own understanding; in all your ways submit to him, and he will make your paths straight." (Proverbs 3:5 – 6)

Repent

To truly repent, you must not only *turn away* from your sins, but *turn toward* God. Repentance allows you to enjoy the freedom of your loving relationship with God.

"Turn from your sins and act on this glorious news!" (Mark 1:15, TLB)

"Don't let the world around you squeeze you into its own mold, but let God remake you so that your whole attitude of mind is changed." (Romans 12:2, PH)

New life

After you ask Jesus into your heart, you will have a new life! You will no longer be bound to your old sin nature. God has declared you NOT GUILTY, and you no longer have to live under the power of sin!

"Now God says he will accept and acquit us — declare us 'not guilty' — if we trust Jesus Christ to take away our sins." (Romans 3:22, TLB)

We will work on the "how tos" of TURNING our life and will over to God in Lesson 6. But do not forget this key point:

Turning your life over to Christ is a once-in-a-lifetime commitment!

Turning your will over to Him requires a daily *re*commitment!

Pray the following prayer daily.

Principle 3 Prayer

Dear God, I have tried to do it all by myself, on my own power, and I have failed. Today, I want to turn my life over to You. I ask You to be my Lord and my Savior. You are the One and only Higher Power! I ask that You help me start to think less about me and my will. I want to daily turn my will over to You, to daily seek Your direction and wisdom for my life. Please continue to help me overcome my hurts, hang-ups, and habits and may that victory over them help others as they see Your power at work in changing my life. Help me to do Your will always. In Jesus' name I pray, Amen.

Write About It

1. What is stopping you from asking Jesus Christ into your heart as your Lord and Savior? (If you have already asked Christ into your life, describe your experience.)

2. How has relying on your "own understanding" caused problems in your life? Be specific.

3. What does "repent" mean to you? What do you need to repent of?

4. What does the declaration of "not guilty" found in Romans 3:22 mean to you?

5. When you turn your life over to your Higher Power, Jesus Christ, you have a "new life" (see 2 Corinthians 5:17). What does that "new life" mean to you?

6. What does the Principle 3 prayer mean to you?

Lesson 6

ACTION

Principle 3: Consciously choose to commit all my life and will to Christ's care and control.

"Happy are the meek." (Matthew 5:5)

Step 3: We made a decision to turn our lives and our wills over to the care of God.

"Therefore, I urge you, brothers and sisters, in view of God's mercy, to offer your bodies as a living sacrifice, holy and pleasing to God — this is your true and proper worship." (Romans 12:1)

Think About It

Even after taking the first two steps we can still be stuck in the cycle of failure: guilt → anger → fear → depression!

How do we get "unstuck"? How do we get past the barriers of pride, fear, guilt, worry, and doubt that keep us from taking this step?

The answer is *we need to take ACTION!*

Accept Jesus Christ as your Higher Power and Savior!

Make the decision to ask Jesus into your heart. Now is the time to commit your life, to establish that personal relationship with Jesus that He so desires.

"If you confess with your mouth, 'Jesus is Lord,' and believe in your heart that God raised him from the dead, you will be saved." (Romans 10:9)

Commit to seek and follow HIS will!

We need to change our definition of willpower: Willpower is the willingness to accept God's power. We see that there is no room for God if we are full of ourselves.

"Teach me to do your will, for you are my God; may your good Spirit lead me on level ground." (Psalm 143:9 – 10)

Turn it over

"Let go; let God!" Turn over all the big things and the little things in your life to your Higher Power. Jesus Christ wants a relationship with *ALL* of you. What burdens are you carrying that you want to *TURN OVER* to God?

"Come to me and I will give you rest — all of you who work so hard beneath a heavy yoke. Wear my yoke — for it fits perfectly — and let me teach you; for I am gentle and humble, and you shall find rest for your souls." (Matthew 11:28 – 30, TLB)

It's only the beginning

In the third principle we make only the initial decision, the commitment to seek and follow God's will. Our walk with our Higher Power, Jesus Christ, begins with this decision and is followed by a lifelong process of growing as a Christian.

"God who began the good work within you will keep right on helping you grow in his grace until his task within is finally finished." (Philippians 1:6, TLB)

One day at a time

Recovery happens one day at a time. If we remain stuck in the yesterday or constantly worry about tomorrow, we will waste the precious time of the present. We can only change our hurts, hang-ups, and habits in the present.

"So don't be anxious about tomorrow. God will take care of your tomorrow too. Live one day at a time." (Matthew 6:34, TLB)

Next: How do I ask Christ into my life?

Ask yourself the following four questions (see box), and if you answer yes to all of them, pray the prayer that follows them. That's it. That's all you have to do!

How to Establish a "Spiritual Base" for My Life
By Pastor Rick Warren

Do I. . .
***B**elieve Jesus Christ died on the cross for me and showed He was God by coming back to life?*
(1 Corinthians 15:2 – 4)

Do I. . .
***A**ccept God's free forgiveness for my sins?*
(Romans 3:22)

Do I. . .
***S**witch to God's plan for my life?*
(Mark 1:16–18; Romans 12:2)

Do I. . .
***E**xpress my desire to Christ to be the director of my life?*
(Romans 10:9)

Dear God, I believe you sent Your Son, Jesus, to die for my sins so I can be forgiven. I'm sorry for my sins and I want to live the rest of my life the way you want me to. Please put Your Spirit in my life to direct me. Amen.

Write About It

1. What differences have you noticed in your life now that you have accepted Jesus Christ as your Higher Power?

2. How has your definition of willpower changed since you have been in recovery?

3. What have you been able to turn over to God?

4. What do you fear turning over to His care?

5. What is keeping you from turning them over?

6. What does the phrase "live one day at a time" mean to you?

7. What is a major concern in your life?

8. What's stopping you from turning it over to your Higher Power, Jesus Christ?

Principle 3 Verses

"If you confess with your mouth, 'Jesus is Lord,' and believe in your heart that God raised him from the dead, you will be saved." (Romans 10:9)

"If you had faith even as small as a tiny mustard seed you could say to this mountain, 'Move!' and it would go far away. Nothing would be impossible." (Matthew 17:20, TLB)

"Come to me and I will give you rest — all of you who work so hard beneath a heavy yoke. Wear my yoke — for it fits perfectly — and let me teach you; for I am gentle and humble, and you shall find rest for your souls; for I give you only light burdens." (Matthew 11:28 – 30, TLB)

"Commit everything you do to the Lord. Trust him to help you do it and he will." (Psalm 37:5, TLB)

"Lead me; teach me; for you are the God who gives me salvation. I have no hope except in you." (Psalm 25:5, TLB)

"Indeed, in our hearts we felt the sentence of death. But this happened that we might not rely on ourselves but on God, who raises the dead." (2 Corinthians 1:9)

"Teach me to do your will, for you are my God; may your good Spirit lead me on level ground." (Psalm 143:10)

"In everything you do, put God first, and he will direct you and crown your efforts with success." (Proverbs 3:6, TLB)

Afterword

Now that you have completed all six lessons in this guide to the best of your ability, CONGRATULATIONS are most definitely in order!

In Principle 1 you faced your denial and admitted that by yourself you were powerless to manage your addictive or compulsive behavior.

"For I know that good itself does not dwell in me, that is, in my sinful nature. For I have the desire to do what is good, but I cannot carry it out." (Romans 7:18)

In Principle 2 you found the hope that God could and would restore you to sanity, and that only He could provide the power for you to recover.

"For God is at work within you, helping you want to obey him, and then helping you do what he wants." (Philippians 2:13, TLB)

And finally, in Principle 3, you were able to take the action, to make the decision to turn your life and your will over to God's care and direction.

"And so, dear brothers, I plead with you to give your bodies to God. Let them be a living sacrifice, holy — the kind he can accept. When you think of what he has done for you, is that too much to ask? (Romans 12:1, TLB)

Now, you are ready to take the next step in your journey on the "Road to Recovery." The next participant's guide deals with facing your past — the good and the bad. Principle 4 can be difficult, but remember you're not going to go through it alone. Your Higher Power, Jesus Christ, and others that He has placed alongside you on your "Road to Recovery" will be with you every step of the way.

ALSO AVAILABLE

CELEBRATE RECOVERY
30
ANNIVERSARY

NIV Celebrate Recovery® Study Bible

The *NIV Celebrate Recovery Study Bible* is a powerful and positive ally. This Bible is based on eight recovery principles found in Jesus' Sermon on the Mount and on the underlying Christ-centered twelve steps of the proven Celebrate Recovery program. Now typeset in Zondervan's exclusive Comfort Print® typeface, this Bible and all of its added content lifts you up and shows you how to walk, step by attainable step, on a path of healing and liberty.

Features:

- The full text of the accurate, readable, and clear New International Version (NIV) translation
- Articles explain eight recovery principles and accompanying Christ-centered twelve steps
- 110 lessons unpack eight recovery principles in practical terms

9780310455257

- Recovery stories offer encouragement and hope
- 30 days of recovery-related readings
- Over 50 full-page biblical character studies are tied to stories from real-life people who have found peace and help with their own hurts, hang-ups, and habits
- Book introductions
- Side-column reference system keyed to Celebrate Recovery's eight recovery principles
- Topical index
- Exclusive Zondervan NIV Comfort Print typeface in 9-point print size

Available now at your favorite bookstore.

ZONDERVAN®

ALSO AVAILABLE

CELEBRATE RECOVERY 30 ANNIVERSARY

Celebrate Recovery®

THE JOURNEY CONTINUES

PARTICIPANT'S GUIDES 5-8

Celebrate Recovery® introduces *The Journey Continues*–four participant's guides designed as a revolutionary, second step study curriculum. This step study is taken after completing *The Journey Begins* (Participant Guides 1-4). By working through the lessons and exercises found in each of the four participant's guides of *The Journey Continues* you will find a deeper sense of true peace and serenity, continue to restore and develop stronger relationships with others and with God, and find deeper freedom from life's hurts, habits, and hang-ups.

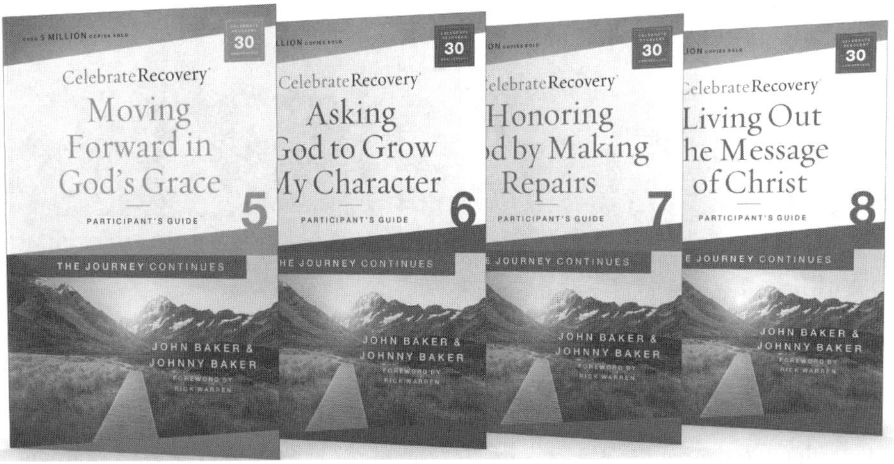

9780310131465 9780310131489 9780310131502 9780310131526

Available now at your favorite bookstore.

ZONDERVAN®

ALSO AVAILABLE

CELEBRATE RECOVERY
30
ANNIVERSARY

Celebrate Recovery®

LEADER'S KIT

For over 30 years, Celebrate Recovery® has helped the church fulfill its role as Christ's healing agent. Since 1991, millions of people have participated in the Celebrate Recovery programs offered at more than 35,000 churches, prisons, and rescue missions in 21 different languages. Developed by John Baker and Rick Warren of Saddleback Church, Celebrate Recovery draws from the Beatitudes to help people overcome their hurts, hang-ups,and habits. Rather than setting up an isolated recovery community, this powerful program helps participants and their churches come together and discover new levels of care, acceptance, trust, and grace.

Leader's Kit: 9780310131601

The 30th anniversary leader's kit includes:

- 1 *Celebrate Recovery Leader's Guide*
- 1 each of *The Journey Begins* participant's guides #1-4
- 1 each of *The Journey Continues* participant's guides #5-8
- 1 Leader's Resource USB stick with 25 editable lessons from *The Journey Begins* curriculum, three videos featuring John Baker, Johnny Baker, and Rick Warren, sermon transcripts, and MP3 sermons.
- 1 *NIV Celebrate Recovery Study Bible*, Comfort Print® edition
- 1 copy of *Your First Step to Celebrate Recovery*
- 1 copy of *Celebrate Recovery 28 Devotions*

Available now at your favorite bookstore.

ZONDERVAN®